the **Bulldog**

A guide to selection, care, nutrition, upbringing, training, health, breeding, sports and play

Contents

Foreword

The book you are holding in your hands right now is by no means a complete book about the Bulldog. If we had collected all the information about the breed, its history and development, feeding, training, health, and whatever else there is to know, this book would have consisted of at least five hundred pages.

What we have done, however, is to bring together all the basic information that you as a (future) owner of an Bulldog need to know in order to handle your pet responsibly. Unfortunately, there are still people who buy a pet without thinking through what they are about to get into.

This book generally deals with the history of the Bulldog, the breed standard and the advantages and disadvantages of buying a Bulldog. It also contains essential information about feeding and about the very first steps in training your dog. Reproduction, day-to-day care, health and breed-specific ailments are also topics.

After having read this book, you can make a carefully considered decision to buy an Bulldog and to keep it as a pet in a responsible manner. We advise you, however, not to rely solely on this book. A well-reared and trained dog is more than just a dog. Invest therefore in a puppy training course or an obedience course. There are also plenty of excellent books that deal with certain aspects, for which we do not have the space in this small book.

About Pets

about pets

A Publication of About Pets.

Copyright © 2003
About Pets
co-publisher United Kingdom
Kingdom Books
PO9 5TL, England

ISBN 1852791845
First printed
December 2004

Original title: *de Engelse bulldog*
© 2004 Welzo Media Productions bv,
About Pets bv,
Warffum, the Netherlands
www.aboutpets.info

Photos:
Rob Dekker, Kingdom Books,
members of the Bulldog Club,
Isabelle Francoise
Fam. Wildhagen,

Printed in China
through Printworks Int. Ltd.

In general

If you have ever looked into the eyes of a Bulldog and have seen the adoration for its master within them, you will understand what B. Quintana meant.

Man's best friend,
The lovely sour snout

When surrounded by cares and in times of need,
Turn to your Bulldog, your friend indeed.
Feeling lonely or just simply tired,
Its love and devotion will have you inspired.

It looks at you, with eyes so quiet,
That follow you watchfully until it's night,
Its devotion asks such little return,
So treat it well, your friend eternal.

Origins

The Bulldog was first mentioned as a breed in 1630, when it was considered most suitable for 'bull baiting'. This 'sport' originated in 1209, when Earl William Warren Lord Stanford saw two bulls fight over a cow. The butcher's dog joined in the fight and attacked one of the bulls. The bull panicked and ran through the village with the relentlessly attacking dog in its wake. The earl was so enraptured by this spectacle, that he ordered the butcher to supply wild bulls once in a while, so that it could be established as a sport. This sport became so popular in England that it lasted 400 years until it was abolished. The English came up with ever-new animals, against which the Bulldog had to fight.

These included horses, bears, donkeys, lions and polar bears.

The English have always been good dog breeders, and it is therefore not surprising that, after Mastiffs were used in the early days, a certain type of dog was needed for bull baiting. In some Mastiff litters, puppies were born with achondroplasia, which is a malformation causing the foetus' cartilage to solidify wrongly. Characteristics are: a big head with a wide skull, in which the lower jaw protrudes in front of the upper jaw, shortened, thick extremities and a carp-back. The bony part of the nose is 'pushed back' quite far. The skin is ample and lies in folds. There are other breeds, such as the Basset, which have been bred from achondroplastic dogs. A side effect of this condition is an increased intelligence. Achondroplasia also occurs in humans.

The Bulldog's specific build has always been determined by its original use. It is quite small, which reduced the risk of the dog being injured by the bull, as it was too small to be hit by the bull's horns. The bull could instead only manage to thrust its head over the dog's back when trying to attack. It has a set-back nose, which enables it to carry on breathing when hanging onto the bull. The skin lies in folds, which minimizes the risk of internal injuries. The Bulldog's character is brave and determined, with a high pain threshold, which was necessary when entering a possibly fatal fight.

When this cruel sport was finally abolished in 1835, the breed quickly declined in numbers and it even seemed that it would become extinct. Dog fights still existed, but terriers were quicker and fiercer. The Bulldog, certainly not a friendly dog at that time, quickly ended up in the underworld. A number of people luckily made the Bulldog the national breed, as it was closely linked to England's history. All possible measures were taken to improve the Bulldog's character, so that this dog would not have to spend its days locked up in a kennel.

The modern Bulldog has become a friendly, good-natured companion. Its almost bourgeois nature, its painstaking attempts at hanging on to familiar things, and its sentimental and especially reliable character, all make it an ideal housemate.

Breed standard
A standard has been developed for all breeds recognised by the FCI (Fédération Cynologique Internationale). The FCI is the umbrella organisation of the Western European dog world. The officially approved breed associations of the member countries provide translations of the breed standard. This standard provides a guideline for breeders and inspectors. It is something of an ideal that dogs of each breed must strive to match. With some breeds, dogs are already being bred that match the ideal. Other breeds have a long way to go. There is a list of defects for each breed. These can be serious defects that disqualify the dog, in which case it will be excluded from breeding. Permitted defects are not serious, but do cost points in a show.

The UK Breed Standard of the Bulldog

General Appearance
Smooth-coated, thick set, rather low in stature, broad, powerful and compact. Head, fairly large in proportion to size but no point so much in excess of others as to destroy the general symmetry, or make the dog appear deformed, or interfere with its powers of motion. Face short, muzzle broad, blunt and inclined upwards. Dogs showing respiratory distress highly undesirable. Body short, well knit, limbs stout, well muscled and in hard condition with no tendency towards obesity. Hindquarters high and strong but somewhat lighter in comparison with heavy foreparts. Bitches not so grand or well developed as dogs.

Characteristics
Conveys impression of determination, strength and activity.

Temperament
Alert, bold, loyal, dependable, courageous, fierce in appearance, but possessed of affectionate nature.

Head and Skull
Skull large in circumference. Viewed from front appears very high from corner of lower jaw to apex of skull; also very broad and square. Cheeks well rounded and extended sideways beyond eyes.

Viewed from side, head appears very high and short from back to point of nose. Forehead flat with skin upon and about head, loose and wrinkled, neither prominent nor overhanging face. Projections of frontal bones prominent, broad, square and high; deep, wide indentation between eyes. From stop, a furrow, both broad and deep extending to middle of skull being traceable to apex. Face from front of cheek bone to nose, short, skin wrinkled. Muzzle short, broad, turned upwards and very deep from corner of eye to corner of mouth. Nose and nostrils large, broad and black, under no circumstances liver colour, red or brown; top set back towards eyes. Distance from inner corner of eye (or from centre of stop between eyes) to extreme tip of nose not exceeding length from tip of nose to edge of underlip. Nostrils large wide and open, with well defined vertical straight line between. Flews (chops) thick, broad, pendant and very deep, hanging completely over lower jaws at sides, not in front, joining underlip in front and quite covering teeth. Jaws broad, massive and square, lower jaw projecting in front of upper and turning up. Nose roll must not interfere with the line of layback. Viewed from front, the various properties of the face must be equally balanced on either side of an imaginary line down centre.

Eyes

Seen from front, situated low down in skull, well away from ears. Eyes and stop in same straight line, at right angles to furrow. Wide apart, but outer corners within the outline of cheeks. Round in shape, of moderate size, neither sunken nor prominent, in colour very dark-almost black - showing no white when looking directly forward. Free from obvious eye problems.

Ears

Set high - i.e. front edge of each ear (as viewed from front) joins outline of skull at top corner of such outline, so as to place them as wide apart, as high and as far from eyes as possible. Small and thin. 'Rose ear' correct, i.e. folding inwards back, upper or front inner edge curving outwards and backwards, showing part of inside of burr.

Mouth

Jaws broad and square with six small front teeth between canines in an even row. Canines wide apart. Teeth large and strong, not seen when mouth closed. When viewed from front under jaw directly under upper jaw and parallel.

Neck

Moderate in length, very thick, deep and strong. Well arched at back, with much loose, thick and wrinkled skin about throat, forming dewlap on each side, from lower jaw to chest.

Forequarters

Shoulders broad, sloping and deep, very powerful and muscular giving appearance of being 'tacked on' body. Brisket capacious, round and very deep from top of shoulders to lowest part where it joins chest. Well let down between forelegs. Large in diameter, round behind forelegs (not flat-sided, ribs well rounded). Forelegs very stout and strong, well developed, set wide apart, thick, muscular and straight, presenting rather bowed outline, but bones of legs large and straight, not bandy nor curved and short in proportion to hindlegs, but not so short as to make back appear long, or detract from dog's activity and so cripple him. Elbows low and standing well away from ribs. Pasterns short, straight and strong.

Body

Chest wide, laterally round, prominent and deep. Back short, strong, broad at shoulders, comparatively narrower at loins. Slight fall to back close behind shoulders (lowest part) whence spine should rise to loins (top higher than top of shoulder), curving again more suddenly to tail, forming arch (termed roach back) - a distinctive characteristic of breed. Body well ribbed up behind with belly tucked up and not pendulous.

Hindquarters

Legs large and muscular, longer in proportion than forelegs, so as to elevate loins. Hocks slightly bent, well let down; legs long and muscular from loins to hock; short, straight, strong lower part. Stifles round and turned slightly outwards away from body. Hocks thereby made to approach each other and hind feet to turn outwards.

Feet

Fore, straight and turning very slightly outward; of medium size and moderately round. Hind, round and compact. Toes compact and thick, well split up, making knuckles prominent and high.

Tail

Set on low, jutting out rather straight and then turning downwards. Round, smooth and devoid of fringe or coarse hair. Moderate in length - rather short than long - thick at root, tapering quickly to a fine point. Downward carriage (not having a decided upward curve at end) and never carried above back.

Gait/Movement

Peculiarly heavy and constrained, appearing to walk with short, quick steps on tips of toes, hind feet not lifted high, appearing to skim ground, running with one or other shoulder rather advanced. Soundness of movement of the utmost importance.

Coat

Fine texture, short, close and smooth (hard only from shortness and closeness, not wiry).

Colour

Whole or smut, (i.e. whole colour with black mask or muzzle). Only whole colours (which should be brilliant and pure of their sort) viz., brindles, reds with their various shades, fawns, fallows etc., white and pied (i.e. combination of white with any of the foregoing colours). Dudley, black and black with tan highly undesirable.

Size

Dogs: 25 kgs (55 lbs); bitches: 23 kgs (50 lbs).

Faults

Any departure from the foregoing points should be considered a fault and the seriousness with which the fault should be regarded should be in exact proportion to its degree and its effect upon the health and welfare of the dog.

Note

Male animals should have two apparently normal testicles fully descended into the scrotum. Produced courtesy of the Kennel Club of Great Britain, September 2003

The Bulldog

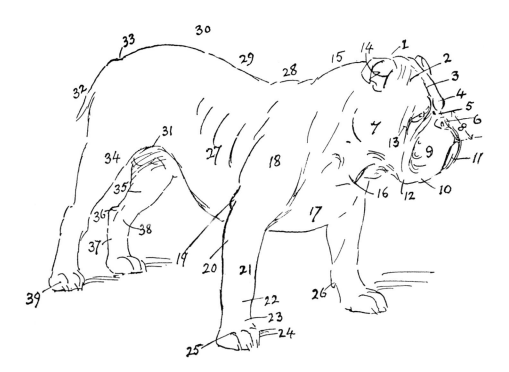

1 occiput	14 point where ear is attached to head	27 ribs
2 skull	15 neck	28 withers
3 furrow	16 dewlap	29 roach back
4 foreface	17 chest	30 loins
5 stop	18 shoulder and upper arm	31 belly
6 nose	19 elbow	32 tail
7 cheek	20 ulna	33 point of tail
8 layback	21 forearm	34 thigh
9 chop	22 wrist	35 lower thigh
10 muzzle	23 pastern	36 heel
11 turn-up	24 toes	37 metatarsal
12 corner of jaw	25 knuckles	38 hock
13 corner of eye	26 stopper pad	39 toes

Buying a Bulldog

Once you've made that properly considered decision to buy a dog, there are several options. Should it be a puppy, an adult dog, or even an older dog? Should it be a bitch or a dog, a pedigree dog or a cross?

Of course, the question also comes up as to where to buy your dog. It is important for you and the animal that you sort out these things in advance. You want to find a dog that fits in with your situation.

With a puppy, you choose a playful, energetic housemate, which will adapt easily to its new surroundings. If you want something a little quieter, an older dog is a good choice.

Advantages and disadvantages of the Bulldog

Bulldogs are friendly towards anyone, and particularly towards children. As far as is known, no healthy, well-bred Bulldog has ever attacked a child. The Bulldog's far-reaching friendliness has its disadvantages, too. The

Bulldog is not a guard dog. Even though burglars come at night, as long as they enter 'normally', they will be welcomed heartily and enthusiastically. If they enter through a window, however, it will be considered 'not normal', and the result will often be loud and worried barking.

The Bulldog will not enjoy accompanying its master on lengthy walks in the woods in summer. This does not mean that it is a dog for lazy people, as is often assumed. Especially young Bulldogs need very well regulated exercise to build up their muscles. Bulldogs can normally cope well with heat, as long as they can lie in the shade. Exercise is a different matter. In warm weather, walks should be limited to a short stroll in the early morning and another one in the late evening.

Dog or bitch?

Whether you choose a male or a female puppy, or an adult dog or bitch, is an entirely personal decision. A male typically needs more leadership because he tends to be more dominant by nature. He will try to play boss over other dogs and, if he gets the chance, over people too. In the wild, the most dominant dog (or wolf) is always the leader of the pack. In many cases this is a male. A bitch is much more focussed on her master, as she sees him as the pack leader.

A puppy test is good for defining what kind of character a young dog will develop. During a test one usually sees that a dog is more dominant than a bitch. You can often quickly recognise the bossy, the adventurous and the cautious characters. So visit the litter a couple of times early on. Try to pick a puppy that suits your own personality. A dominant dog, for instance, needs a strong hand. It will often try to see how far it can go. You must regularly make it clear who's the boss, and that it must obey all the members of the family.

When bitches are sexually mature, they will go into season. On average, a bitch is in season twice a year for about two or three weeks. This is the fertile period when she can become pregnant. Particularly in the second half of her season, she will want to go looking for a dog to mate with. A male dog will show more masculine traits once he is sexually mature. He will make sure other dogs know what territory is his by urinating as often as possible in as many places as he can. He will also be difficult to restrain if there's a bitch in season nearby. As far as normal care is concerned, there is little difference between a dog and a bitch.

Puppy or adult dog?

After you've made the decision for a male or a female, the next question comes up. Should it be a puppy or an adult dog? Your household circumstances usually play a major role here.

Of course, it's great having a sweet little puppy in the house, but bringing up a young dog costs a lot of time. In the first year of its life it learns more than during the rest of its life. This is the period when the foundations are laid for elementary matters, such as house-training, obedience and social behaviour. You must reckon with the fact that your puppy will keep you busy for a couple of hours a day, certainly in the first few months. You won't need so much time with a grown dog. It has already been brought up, but

this doesn't mean it doesn't need correcting from time to time.

A puppy will no doubt leave a trail of destruction in its wake for the first few months. With a little luck, this will only cost you a number of rolls of wallpaper, some good shoes and a few socks. In the worst case you'll be left with some chewed furniture. Some puppies even manage to tear curtains from their rails. With good upbringing this 'vandalism' will quickly disappear, but you won't have to worry about this if you get an older dog.

The greatest advantage of a puppy, of course, is that you can bring it up your own way. And the upbringing a dog gets (or doesn't get) is a major influence on its whole character. Finally, financial aspects may play a role in your decision. A puppy is generally (much) more expensive than an adult dog, not only in purchase price but also in 'maintenance'. A puppy needs to go to the vet's more often for the necessary vaccinations and check-ups.

Overall, bringing up a puppy costs a good deal of energy, time and money, but you have its upbringing in your own hands. An adult dog costs less money and time, but its character has already been formed. You should also try to find out about the background of an adult dog. Its previous owner may have formed its character in somewhat less positive ways.

Two dogs?

Having two or more dogs in the house is not just nice for us, but also for the animals themselves. Dogs get a lot of pleasure from company of their own kind. After all, they are pack animals.

If you're sure that you want two young dogs, it's best not to buy them at the same time. Bringing a dog up and establishing the bond between dog and master takes time, and you need to give a lot of attention to your dog in this phase. Having two puppies in the house means you have to divide your attention between them. Apart from that, there's a danger that they will focus on one another rather than on their master. Buy the second pup when the first is (almost) an adult. However, two adult dogs can easily be brought into the home at the same time.

Getting a puppy when the first dog is somewhat older often has a positive effect on the older dog. The influence of the puppy almost seems to give it a second childhood. The older dog, if it's been well brought up, can help with the upbringing of the puppy. Dogs like to imitate each other's behaviour. Don't forget to give both dogs the same amount of

attention. Take the puppy out alone at least once per day during the first eighteen months. Make sure the older dog has enough opportunity to get some peace and quiet. It won't always be able to keep up with the speed of such an enthusiastic youngster.

It is inadvisable to keep two male Bulldogs together. Male Bulldogs are too dominant to live together. For the first eighteen months they will pretend that everything is fine. But just when you lean back satisfied, because you think that you have succeeded after all, they attack each other and can no longer be kept in the same room.

The combination of a male and a female needs special attention. If you don't plan to breed with your dogs, now or ever, then you should take measures to make sure this doesn't happen. Besides sterilising a female, males can also be castrated, but this is normally only done for medical reasons or to solve behaviour problems.

A dog and children
Dogs and children are a great combination. They can play together and get great pleasure out of each other's company. Moreover children need to learn how to handle living beings; they develop respect and a sense of responsibility by caring for a dog (or another pet).

However sweet a dog is, children must understand that it is an animal and not a toy. A dog isn't comfortable when it's being messed around with. So make it

clear what a dog likes and what it doesn't. Look for ways the child can play with the dog, perhaps a game of hide-and-seek where the child hides and the dog has to find it. Even a simple tennis ball can give enormous pleasure. Children must learn to leave a dog in peace when it doesn't want to play any more. The dog must also have its own place where it's not disturbed. Have children help with your dog's care as much as possible. A strong bond will be the result.

The arrival of a baby also means changes in the life of a dog. Before the birth you can help get the dog acquainted with the new situation. Let it sniff at the new things in the house and it will quickly accept them. When the baby has arrived, involve the dog as much as possible in day-by-day events, but make sure it gets plenty of attention too.

Never leave a dog alone with young children! Crawling infants sometimes make unexpected

movements, which can easily frighten a dog. And infants are hugely curious, and may try to find out whether the tail is really fastened to the dog, or whether its eyes come out, just like they do with their cuddly toys. But a dog is a dog and it will defend itself when it feels threatened.

Where to buy

There are various ways of acquiring a dog. The decision for a puppy or an adult dog will also define for the most part where you buy your dog.

If it's to be a puppy, then you need to find a breeder with a litter. If you are planning to buy an Bulldog, it is important to go to a breeder who is known for breeding nice and, most importantly, healthy dogs. It should also 'click' between breeder and buyer. This is important because you are about to buy a living being and, although the breeder might give his best, there can always be something wrong with a puppy. Being on good terms with the breeder is therefore essential, so

that you can always go back there if you encounter a problem.

If you choose a popular breed, such as the Bulldog, there is choice enough. But you may also face the problem that there are so many puppies on sale that have only been bred for profit's sake or that have even been imported from eastern Europe. You can see how many puppies are for sale by looking in the regional newspaper every Saturday. Some of these dogs have a real pedigree, but many don't. Breeders often don't watch out for breed-specific illnesses and in-breeding; puppies are separated from their mother as fast as possible and are thus insufficiently socialised. Never buy a puppy that is too young, or whose mother you weren't able to see. Always buy a puppy via the breed association.

Fortunately there are also enough bona-fide breeders of Bulldogs. Try to visit a number of breeders before you actually buy your puppy. Ask if the breeder is prepared to help you after you've bought your puppy, and to help you find solutions for any problems that may come up. To bring together breeders and potential buyers of puppies, many breed clubs provide information on recent litters.

Finally, you must realise that a pedigree is nothing more or less

than a proof of descent. The Kennel Club also issues pedigrees to the young of parents that suffer from congenital conditions, or that have never been checked for these. A pedigree says nothing about the health of the parent dogs. If you buy your puppy via the breed association, you can be sure that the breeder adhered to the association's breeding rules. These include health requirements for breeding animals.

If you would prefer to buy an adult dog, you can contact the breed association. They sometimes help with re-homing adult dogs, which can no longer be kept by their owners due to circumstances (such as impulse buying, moving home or divorce).

What to watch out for

Buying a puppy is no simple matter. You must pay attention to the following:

- Never buy a puppy on impulse, even if it is love at first sight. A dog is a living being that will need a lot of care and attention over a long period (nine to eleven years!). It is not a toy that you can put away when you're done with it.
- Take a good look at the mother. Is she calm, nervous, aggressive, well cared-for or neglected? The behaviour and condition of the mother is not only a sign of the quality of the breeder, but also of the puppy you're about to buy.
- Avoid buying a puppy whose mother has been kept only in a kennel. A young dog needs as many different impressions as possible in its first few months, including living in a family group. It gets used to people and possibly other pets. Kennel dogs miss these experiences and are inadequately socialised.
- Always ask to see the parents' papers (vaccination certificates, pedigrees, official health examination certificates).
- Never buy a puppy younger than eight weeks.
- Put all agreements with the breeder in writing. A model agreement is available from the breed association.
- Ask if the breeder participates in health monitoring in association with the breed association.

Travelling with your Bulldog

There are a few things to think about before travelling with your dog. While one dog may enjoy travelling, another may hate it.

While you might enjoy going on holidays to far-away places, it is questionable whether your dog does, too.

That very first trip
The first trip of a puppy's life is also the most nerve-wrecking. This is the trip from the breeder's to its new home.

If possible, pick up your puppy in the morning. It then has the whole day to get used to the new situation. Ask the breeder not to feed the puppy that day. The young animal will be overwhelmed by all kinds of new experiences. Firstly, it's away from its mother; it's in a small room (the car) with all its different smells, noises and strange people. So there's a big chance that the puppy will be car-sick this first time, with the annoying consequence that it

will remember travelling in the car as an unpleasant experience. So it's important to make this first trip as pleasant as possible.

When picking up your puppy, always take someone with you who can sit in the back seat with the puppy on his or her lap and talk to it calmly. If it's too warm for the puppy, a place on the floor at the feet of your companion is ideal. The pup will lie there relatively quietly and may even take a nap. Ask the breeder for a cloth or something else from its nest, which carries a familiar scent. The puppy can lie on this in the car, and it will also help if it feels lonely during the first nights at home.

If the trip home is a long one, then stop for a break (once in a while). Let your puppy roam and sniff around (on the lead!), have a little drink and, if necessary, let it do its business. Do take care to lay an old towel in the car. It can happen that the puppy, in its nervousness, may urinate or be sick.

It's also good advice to give a puppy positive experiences with car journeys as soon as possible. Make short trips to nice places where you can walk and play with it. It can be a real nuisance if your dog doesn't like travelling in a car.

Taking your Bulldog on holidays

When making holiday plans, you also need to think about what you're going to do with your dog during that time. Are you taking it with you, putting it into kennels or

leaving it with friends? In any event there are a number of things you need to do in good time.

If you want to take your dog with you, you need to be sure in advance that it will be welcome at your holiday home, and what the rules there are. If you're going abroad it will need certain vaccinations and a health certificate, which normally need to be done four weeks before departure. You must also be sure that you've made all the arrangements necessary to bring your dog back home to the UK, without it needing to go into quarantine under the rabies regulations. Your vet can give you the most recent information. If your trip is to southern Europe,

ask your vet for a treatment against ticks (you can read more about this in the *Parasites* chapter).

Although dog-owners usually enjoy taking their dog on holiday, you must seriously ask yourself whether the dog feels that way too. Bulldogs certainly don't always feel comfortable in a hot country. Days spent travelling in a car are also often not their preference, and some dogs suffer badly from car-sickness. There are good medicines for this, but it's questionable whether you're doing your dog a favour with them.

If you do decide to take it with you, make regular stops at safe places during your journey, so that your dog can have a good run. Take plenty of fresh drinking water with you, as well as enough of the food your dog is used to. Don't leave your dog in the car standing in the sun. It can quickly be overcome by the heat, which can have fatal consequences.

If you're travelling by plane or ship, make sure in good time that your dog can travel with you and what rules you need to observe. You will need some time to make all the arrangements. Maybe you decide not to take your dog with you, and you then need to find somewhere for it to stay. Arrangements for a place in kennels need to be made well in advance. There are special kennels for Bulldogs. There will be certain vaccinations required, which need to be given a minimum of one month before the stay. If your dog can't be accommodated in the homes of relatives or friends, it might be possible to have an acquaintance stay in your house. This also needs to be arranged well in advance, as it may be difficult to find someone who can do this.

Always ensure that your dog can be traced should it run away or get lost while on holiday. A little tube with your address, or a tag with home and holiday address, can avoid a lot of problems.

Moving home
Dogs generally become more attached to humans than to the house they live in. Moving home is usually not a problem for them. But it can be useful to let the dog get to know its new home and the area around it before moving.

If you can, leave your dog somewhere else (with relatives, friends, or in kennels) on the day of the move. The chance of it running away or getting lost is then practically non-existent. Once you have completed your move, you

can pick your dog up and let it quietly get familiar with its new home and environment. Give it its own place in the house at once and it will quickly adapt. During the first week or so, always walk your dog on a lead, because an animal can get lost in new surroundings too. Always take a different route so it quickly gets to know the neighbourhood.

Don't forget to get your new address and phone number engraved on your dog's tag. Send a change of address notice to the institution that has any chip or tattoo data. Dogs must sometimes be registered in a new community (just as people), and you must pay for a dog licence. In some communities, you get part of your fee back if you move within the year you paid for.

Feeding your Bulldog

A dog will actually eat a lot more than just meat. In the wild it would eat its prey complete with skin and fur, including the bones, stomach, and the innards with their semi-digested vegetable material.

In this way the dog supplements its meat menu with the vitamins and minerals it needs. This is also the basis for feeding a domestic dog.

Ready-made foods

It's not easy for a layman to put together a complete menu for a dog, including all the necessary proteins, fats, vitamins and minerals in just the right proportions and quantities. Meat alone is certainly not a complete meal for a dog, as it contains too little calcium. A continuous calcium deficiency will lead to bone defects, and for a fast-growing puppy this can lead to serious skeletal deformities. If you put its food together yourself, you can easily give your dog too much in terms of vitamins and minerals, which can also be bad for your dog's health.

You can avoid these problems by giving it ready-made food of a good brand. These products are well balanced and contain everything your dog needs. Supplements, such as vitamin preparations, are superfluous. The amount of food your dog needs depends on its weight and activity level. You can find guidelines on the packaging. Split the food into two meals per day if possible, and always ensure that there's a dish of fresh drinking water next to its food.

Give your dog the time to digest its food and don't let it outside straight after a meal. A dog should never play on a full stomach. This can cause stomach torsion (the stomach turning over), which can be fatal for your dog.

Because the food needs of a dog depend, among other things, on its age and way of life, there are many different types of dog food available. There are "light" foods for less active dogs, "energy" foods for working dogs and "senior" foods for the older dog.

There is now a wide assortment of puppy foods available. These foods contain higher amounts of growth-promoting nutrients, such as proteins and calcium. Thus only feed your puppy special puppy food.

Canned foods, mixers and dry foods

Ready-made foods, which are available at pet shops or in the supermarket, can roughly be split into canned food, mixer and dry food. Whichever form you choose, ensure that it's a complete food with all the necessary nutrients. You can see this on the packaging. Most dogs love canned food. Although the better brands are composed well, they do have one disadvantage: they are soft. A dog fed only on canned food will sooner or later have problems with its teeth (plaque, paradontosis). Besides canned food, give your dog hard foods or dog chews at certain times.

Mixer is a food consisting of chunks, dried vegetables and grains. Almost all the moisture has been extracted. The advantages of mixer are that it is light and keeps well. You add a certain amount of water and the meal is ready. A disadvantage is that it must definitely not be fed without water. Without the extra fluid, mixer will absorb the fluids present in the stomach, which can cause serious problems. Should your dog manage to get at the bag and enjoy its contents, you must immediately give it plenty to drink.

Dry foods have also had moisture extracted, but not as much as mixer. The advantage of dry foods is that they are hard, forcing the dog to use its jaws, removing plaque and massaging the gums.

Dog chew products

Naturally, once in a while you want to spoil your dog with something extra. Don't give it pieces of cheese or sausage as these contain too much salt and fat. There are various products available that a dog will find delicious and which are also healthy, especially for its teeth. You'll find a large range of varying quality in the pet shop.

Cowhide and buffalo hide chews

Bulldogs must never be given dog chews made of cowhide or buffalo hide. Because this breed has an undershot lower jaw, its teeth do not sit on each other. It finds it therefore very difficult to bite off pieces of cowhide or buffalo hide.

Your Bulldog will chew the whole chew until it's soft and then try to swallow it whole, which can cause choking and suffocation.

The butcher's left-overs

The bones of slaughtered animals have traditionally been given to the dog, and dogs are crazy about them, but they are not without risks. Pork and poultry bones are too weak. They can splinter and cause serious injury to the intestines. Beef bones are more suitable, but they must first be cooked to kill off dangerous bacteria. Pet shops carry a range of smoked, cooked and dried abattoir residue, such as pigs' ears, bull penis, tripe sticks, oxtails, gullet, dried muscle meat, and hoof chews.

Munchie sticks

Fresh meat

If you do want to give your dog fresh meat occasionally, never give it raw, but always boiled or roasted. Raw (or not fully cooked) pork or chicken can contain life-threatening bacteria. Chicken can be contaminated by the notorious salmonella bacteria, while pork

can carry the Aujeszky virus. This disease is incurable and will quickly lead to your pet's death.

Munchie sticks

Munchie sticks are green, yellow, red or brown coloured sticks of various thicknesses. They consist of ground buffalo hide with a number of often undefined additives. Dogs usually love them because these sticks have been dipped in the blood of slaughtered animals. The composition and quality of these between-meal treats is not always clear. Some are fine, but there have also been sticks found to contain high levels of cardboard and even paint residues. Choose a product whose ingredients are clearly labelled.

Overweight?

Recent investigations have shown that many dogs are overweight. A dog usually becomes too fat because of over-feeding and lack of exercise. Use of medicines, or a disease, is rarely the cause. Dogs that become too fat are often given too much food or too many treats between meals. Gluttony or boredom can also be a cause, and a dog often puts on weight following castration or sterilisation. Due to changes in hormone levels it becomes less active and consumes less energy. Finally, simply too little exercise alone can lead to a dog becoming overweight.

You can use the following rule of thumb to check whether your Bulldog is overweight: you should be able to feel its ribs, but not see them. If you can't feel its ribs then your dog is much too fat.

Overweight dogs live a passive life, they play too little and tire quickly. They also suffer from all kinds of medical problems (problems in joints and heart conditions). They usually die younger too. So it's important to make sure that your dog doesn't become too fat. Always follow the guidelines on food packaging. Adapt them if your dog is less active or gets lots of snacks. Try to make sure your dog gets plenty of exercise by playing and running with it as much as you can. If your dog starts to show signs of putting on weight, you can switch to a low-calorie food. If it's really too fat and reducing its food quantity doesn't help, then a special diet is the only solution.

Caring for your Bulldog

Good (daily) care is extremely important for your dog. A well cared-for dog is less likely to become ill. Caring for your dog is not only necessary but also a pleasure, as master and dog give each other all their attention.

It is also a good moment for playing and cuddling.

Coat

A healthy Bulldog has a shiny coat, which should be brushed once a week with a rubber massage brush. It is advisable to get a puppy used to being brushed from an early age, and to brush it every day, as 'Start 'em young!' applies to dogs too.

Brushing your dog every week should make bathing superfluous. If, however, your dog had a good roll in something unpleasant, then wash it with a special dog shampoo. The acidity level of your dog's skin is different to that of human skin. Special dog shampoos take account of this.

Skin folds

The skin folds in the Bulldog's face need to be checked at least once a week and need to be cleaned with a dry tissue. If the skin folds at the eyes are darker, it is due to excess tear gland discharge. You can smear Vaseline into the fold, so that the discharge doesn't get a chance to stick to the hairs. If the eye folds are very red, you can use zinc salve. The skin fold at the nose needs to be kept dry, too.

Teeth

A Bulldog generally has few problems with its teeth, although it might suffer from tartar and bad breath when it gets older. To prevent this, you should have the teeth checked for tartar when taking your dog to the vet's for its annual vaccinations. Bad breath can be the result of dental problems. Therefore regularly feed your dog hard feed, or provide it with something to chew, and brush its teeth regularly with a special toothbrush for dogs. Bad breath can also be caused by stomach problems or certain foods. It is then advisable to switch to a different diet.

Nails

On a dog that regularly walks on hard surfaces, the nails usually grind themselves down. In this case there's no need to clip its nails. But it wouldn't do any harm

to check their length now and again, especially on older dogs. If nails are too long, they can cause splayed feet. They then need to be clipped back. Only cut into the white part of the nail, as the red part contains the blood vessels. If you cut the nail too far back, it will bleed profusely. In the case of black nails, it is best to let the vet do this job.

Tail

Some Bulldogs have a curled tail. You will then need to check that there is no dirt underneath. Here too, clean it with a dry cloth and use zinc salve on skin abrasions. Homeopathic sulphur powder can also be useful.

Ears

People often forget the ears when caring for their dogs, but they must be checked at least once a week. If your dog's ears are very dirty or have too much wax, you must clean them. This should preferably be done with a soft cloth, moistened with some oil. Never penetrate the ear canal with an object.

A dog that is constantly shaking its head or scratching at its ears might be suffering from dirty ears, an ear infection or ear mites, which makes a visit to the vet essential.

Bringing up your Bulldog

It is very important that your dog is well brought up and obedient. It makes your dog's company not only more pleasant for you, but also for your environment. A puppy can learn in a playful manner what it might do and what it must never do.

The dog shouldn't be allowed on the couch

Rewarding and being consistent are important tools when bringing up a dog. If you reward good behaviour with your voice, a cuddle or a treat, your dog will quickly learn to obey you. A puppy training course can also help to show you the right way.

(Dis)obedience

Bulldogs are intelligent dogs. Never listen to anyone telling you that Bulldogs will never listen and are too stubborn to learn anything. A Bulldog will do anything for you, as long as it considered it carefully first. You cannot yell at your Bulldog if you want it to obey, but you must encourage it with an enthusiastic voice. Make it feel that it is an honour for it to do something for you. There are

Bulldogs that have achieved the highest obedience diplomas with the help of their enthusiastic owners.

A dog that won't obey you is not just a problem for you, but also for your surroundings. It's therefore important to avoid unwanted behaviour. In fact, this is what training your dog is all about, so get started early. Once again, 'Start 'em young!' should be your motto. An untrained dog is not just a nuisance, but can also cause dangerous situations by running into the road, chasing joggers or jumping at people. A dog must be trained out of this undesirable behaviour as quickly as possible. The longer you let it go on, the more difficult it will become to correct. The best thing to do is to attend a special obedience course. This won't only help to correct the dog's behaviour, but its owner also learns how to handle undesirable behaviour at home. A dog must not only obey its master during training, but at home too.

Always be consistent when training good behaviour and correcting annoying behaviour. This means a dog may always behave in a certain way, or must never behave that way. Reward it for good behaviour and never punish it after the fact for any wrongdoing. If your dog finally comes after you've been calling it a long time, then reward it. If you're angry because you had to wait so long, it may feel it's actually being punished for coming. It will probably not obey at all the next time for fear of punishment.

Try to take no notice of undesirable behaviour. Your dog will perceive your reaction (even a negative one) as a reward for this behaviour. If you do need to correct your dog, then do it immediately. Use your voice or grip it by the scruff of the neck and push it to the ground. This is the way a bitch calls her pups to order. Rewards for good behaviour are, by far, preferable to punishment; they always achieve a better result.

House-training
The very first training (and one of the most important) that a dog needs is house-training. The basis for good house-training is keeping a good eye on your puppy. If you pay attention, you will notice that it will sniff a long time and turn around a certain spot before doing its business there. Pick it up gently and place it outside, always at the same place. Reward it abundantly if it does its business there.

Another good moment for house-training is after it has been eating or sleeping. A puppy often needs to do its business at these times. Let it relieve itself before playing with it, otherwise it will forget to do so and you'll not reach your goal. For the first few days, take your puppy out for a walk just after it's eaten or woken up. It will quickly learn the meaning, especially if it's rewarded with a dog biscuit for a successful attempt. Of course, it's not always possible to go out after every snack or snooze. Lay newspapers at different spots in the house. Whenever the pup needs to do its business, place it on a newspaper. After some time it will start to look for a place itself. Then start to reduce the number of newspapers until there is just one left, at the front or back door. The puppy will learn to go to the door if it needs to relieve itself. Then you put it on the lead and go out

with it. Finally you can remove the last newspaper. Your puppy is now house-trained.

One thing that certainly won't work is punishing an accident after the fact. A dog whose nose is rubbed in its urine or its droppings won't understand that at all. It will only get frightened of you. Rewarding works much better than punishment. An indoor kennel or cage can be a good tool to help in house-training. A puppy won't foul its own nest, so a kennel can be a good solution for the night, or during periods in the day when you can't watch it. But a kennel must not become a prison where your dog is locked up day and night.

First exercises

The basic commands for an obedient dog are those for sit, lie down, come and stay. You can teach a pup to sit by holding a piece of dog biscuit above its nose and then slowly moving it backwards. The puppy's head will also move backwards until its hind legs slowly go down. At that moment you call 'Sit!'. After a few attempts, it will quickly know this nice game. Use the 'Sit!' command before you give your dog its food, put it on the lead, or before it's allowed to cross the street.

Teaching the command to lie down is similar. Instead of moving the piece of dog biscuit backwards, move it down vertically until your hand reaches the ground and then forwards. The dog will also move its forepaws forwards and lie down on its own. At that moment call 'Lie down!' or 'Lay!'. This command is useful when you want a dog to be quiet.

Two people are needed for the 'Come!' command. One holds the dog back while the other runs away. After about fifteen metres, he stops and enthusiastically calls 'Come!'. The other person now lets the dog free, and it should obey the command at once. Again you reward it abundantly. The 'Come!' command is useful in many situations and good for safety too.

A dog learns to stay from the sitting or lying position. While it's sitting or lying down, you call the

At a puppy course

command 'Stay!' and then step back one step. If the dog moves with you, quietly put it back in position, without displaying anger. If you do react angrily, you're actually punishing it for coming to you, and you'll only confuse your dog. It can't understand that coming is rewarded one time, and punished another. Once the dog stays nicely, reward it abundantly. Practice this exercise with increasing distances (at first no more than one metre). The 'Stay!' command is useful when getting out of the car.

Your Bulldog is a very intelligent dog and is happy to do anything for you, as long as you 'talk it through' with it in an enthusiastic manner, and as long as you do not

expect it to react immediately to what you have asked it to do. As soon as you make demands or become impatient, your Bulldog will stop obeying.

Courses

Obedience courses to help you bring up your dog are available across the country. These courses are not just informative, but also fun for dog and master. With a puppy, you can begin with a puppy course. This is designed to provide the basic training. A puppy that has attended such a course has learned about all kinds of things that will confront it in later life: other dogs, humans, traffic and what these mean. The puppy will also learn obedience and to follow a number of basic commands. Apart from all that, attention will be given to important subjects such as brushing, being alone, travelling in a car, and doing its business in the right places.

The next step after a puppy course is a course for young dogs. This course repeats the basic exercises and ensures that the growing dog doesn't get into bad habits. After this, the dog can move on to an obedience course for full-grown dogs.

For more information on where to find courses in your area, contact your local kennel club. You can get its address from the Kennel Club of Great Britain in London. In some areas, the RSPCA organises obedience classes and your local branch may be able to give you information.

Play and toys

There are various ways to play with your dog. You can romp and run with it, but also play a number of games, such as retrieving, tug-of-war, hide-and-seek and catch. A dummy is ideal for retrieving, and you can play tug-of-war with an old sock or a special tugging rope.

Start with tug-of-war only when your dog is a year old. A puppy must first get its second teeth and then they need several months to strengthen. There's a real chance of your dog's teeth becoming

deformed if it starts playing tug-of-war too soon. You can use almost anything for a game of hide-and-seek. Never use too small a ball for games. It can easily get lodged into the dog's throat.

Play is extremely important. Not only does it strengthen the bond between dog and master, but it's also healthy for both. Make sure that you're the one that ends the game. Only stop when the dog has brought back the ball or frisbee, and make sure you always win the tug-of-war. This confirms your dominant position in the hierarchy. Use these toys only during play, so that the dog doesn't forget their significance.

When choosing a special dog toy, remember that dogs are rarely careful with them. So always buy toys of good quality, which a dog can't easily destroy. Be very careful with sticks and twigs. The latter, particularly, can easily splinter. A splinter of wood in your dog's throat or intestines can cause awful problems. Throwing sticks or twigs can also be dangerous. If they stick into the ground, a dog can easily run into them with an open mouth.

Socialisation

If your dog behaves in a reserved and distant manner, the reason for this behaviour can usually be found in the first few weeks of its

It is important that
your puppy has as
many different
experiences as
possible

life. A lack of new experiences in this very important so-called 'socialisation phase' has a big influence on the adult dog's behaviour. If a dog does not get to see humans, other dogs or other animals, it will be distant later. This distance is common with Bulldogs that have grown up in a barn or kennel with very little human contact. It is very important that a dog gets as many new experiences as possible during its first few weeks. Take it into town in the car or on the bus, walk down a busy street with it and let it have plenty of contact with people, other dogs and other animals.

It's a huge task to turn an anxious, poorly socialised dog into a real pet. It will probably take an enormous amount of attention, love, patience and energy to get such an animal used to everything around it. Reward it often and give it plenty of time to adapt and, over time, it will learn to trust you and become less anxious. Try not to force anything, because that will always have the reverse effect. Here too, an obedience course can help a lot. Have visitors give it something tasty as a treat. Put a can of dog biscuits by the door, so that your visitors can spoil your dog when they arrive. Here again, don't try to force anything. If the dog is still frightened, leave it in peace.

Dogs are often frightened in

certain situations; well-known examples are thunderstorms and fireworks. In these cases try to ignore your dog's anxious behaviour. If you react to its whimpering and whining, it's the same as rewarding it. If you ignore its fear completely, the dog will quickly learn that nothing is wrong. You can speed up this 'learning process' by rewarding its positive behaviour.

Rewarding

Rewarding forms the basis for bringing up a dog. Rewarding good behaviour works far better than punishing bad behaviour, and rewarding is also much more fun. Over time the opinions on how to bring up dogs have gradually changed. In the past, a sharp pull on the lead was considered the appropriate way to correct bad behaviour. Today, experts view rewards as a positive incentive to get dogs to do what we expect of them.

There are many ways of rewarding a dog. The usual ways are a stroke or a friendly word, even without a tasty treat to go with it. When bringing up a puppy, a tasty treat at the right moment will work wonders, though. Make sure that you always have something tasty in your pocket to reward it for good behaviour. Another form of reward is play. If a dog realises that you have a ball in your pocket, it won't go far from your side. As soon as you've finished playing, put the ball away. This way your dog will always do its best in exchange for a game.

Despite the emphasis you put on rewarding good behaviour, a dog can sometimes be a nuisance or disobedient. You must correct such behaviour immediately. Always be consistent: once 'no' must always be 'no'.

Barking

Dogs that bark too much are a nuisance for their surroundings. A dog-owner may tolerate barking up to a point, but neighbours are often annoyed by the unnecessary noise. Don't encourage your puppy to bark and yelp. Of course, it should be able to announce its presence, but if it goes on barking it must be called to order with a strict 'Quiet!'.

A dog will sometimes bark for long periods when left alone. It feels threatened and tries to get someone's attention by barking. There are special training programmes for this problem, where a dog learns that being alone is nothing to be afraid of, and that its master will always return. You can practise this with your dog at home. Leave the room and come back in at once. Reward your dog if it stays quiet. Gradually increase the length of your absences and keep rewarding it as long as it remains quiet. Never punish your dog if it does bark or yelp. It will never understand punishment afterwards, and this will only make the problem worse. Never go back into the room as long as your dog is barking, as it will view this as a reward.

You might want to make your dog feel more comfortable by switching the radio on for company during your absence. It will eventually learn that you always come back and the barking will reduce. If you don't get the required result, attend an obedience course.

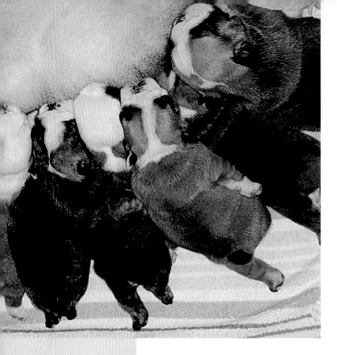

Reproductio

Dogs, and thus also Bulldogs, follow their instincts, and reproduction is one of nature's most important processes. For people who enjoy breeding dogs this is a positive circumstance.

Those who simply want a 'cosy companion' however, will miss the regular adventures with females on heat and unrestrainable males like a toothache. But knowing a little about reproduction in dogs will help you to understand why they behave the way they do, and what measures you need to take when this happens.

Liability
Breeding dogs is much more than simply 1+1= many. If you're planning to breed with your Bulldog, be on your guard. The whole affair can quite easily turn into a financial disaster, because, under the law, a breeder is liable for the 'quality' of his puppies. The kennel clubs place strict conditions on animals used for breeding (see the chapter "Your

Bulldog's health"). If you want to breed a litter for fun, but do not have the relevant experience, you can ask the breed association for advice. Be extremely careful, because, if the puppies you breed show any hereditary abnormalities in later life, you can be held liable by the new owners for any costs arising from any inherited defects. These (veterinary) costs can be enormous! So contact the breeder of your bitch or the breed association if you plan to breed a litter of Bulldogs.

The female in season
It is a myth that it is better for a bitch's health to produce a litter. It is better for most bitches not to have any young! Bitches become sexually mature at about eight to twelve months. Then they go into

season for the first time. They are 'on heat' for two to three weeks. During this period they discharge little drops of blood and they are very attractive to males. The bitch is fertile during the second half of her season, and will accept a male to mate. The best time for mating is then between the ninth and thirteenth day of her season.

A female's first season is often shorter and less severe than those that follow. If you do want to breed with your bitch, you must allow the first and the second season to pass. Most bitches go into season twice per year. If you do plan to breed with your Bulldog in the future, then sterilisation is not an option to prevent unwanted offspring. A temporary solution is a contraceptive injection, although this is controversial because of side effects such as womb infections.

Phantom pregnancy

A phantom pregnancy is a not uncommon occurrence. The female behaves as if she is carrying a litter. She takes all kinds of things to her basket and treats them like puppies. Her milk teats swell and sometimes milk is actually produced. The female will sometimes behave aggressively towards people or other animals, as if she is defending her young. Phantom pregnancies usually begin two

months after a season and can last a number of weeks. If it happens to a bitch once, it will often re-occur after every season. If she suffers under it, sterilisation is the best solution, because repeated phantom pregnancies increase the risk of womb or teat conditions.

In the short term a hormone treatment is worth trying, perhaps also homeopathic medicines. Camphor spirit can give relief when teats are heavily swollen, but rubbing the teats with ice or a cold cloth (moisten and freeze) can also help relieve the pain. Feed her less than usual, and make sure she gets enough distraction and extra exercise.

Preparing to breed

If you do plan to breed a litter of puppies, you must first wait for your female to be physically and mentally full-grown. In any event, you must wait until her third season. To mate a bitch, you need a male. You could simply let her out on the street and she would quickly return home pregnant. But if you have a purebred Bulldog, then it certainly makes sense to mate her with the best possible candidate. Be meticulous with your preparations.

Think especially about the following: Accompanying a bitch through pregnancy, birth and the first eight to twelve weeks afterwards is a time-consuming

affair. The first couple of weeks are a day-and-night job with the Bulldog! Never mate Bulldogs that have congenital defects. The same goes for hyperactive, nervous and shy dogs. If your Bulldog does have a pedigree, then mate her with a dog that also has one. For more information, contact the breed association. You can also go to a dog show and have a look at the dogs on display there, and potentially also their offspring.

Pregnancy

It's often difficult to tell at first if a bitch is pregnant. Only after about four weeks can you feel the pups in her belly. She will now slowly become fatter and her behaviour will usually change. Her teats will swell during the last few weeks of pregnancy.

The average pregnancy lasts 63 days and costs the bitch a lot of energy. In the beginning she is fed her normal amount of food, but her nutritional needs increase in jumps during the second half of the pregnancy. Give her approximately fifteen percent more food each week from the fifth week on. The mother-to-be needs extra energy and proteins during this phase of her pregnancy. During the last weeks you can give her a concentrated food, which is rich in energy, such as dry puppy food. Divide this into several small portions per day, as she can no longer deal with large portions of food. Towards the end of the pregnancy, her energy needs can easily be one-and-a-half times more than usual.

After about seven weeks the mother-to-be will start to demonstrate nesting behaviour and to look for a place to give birth to her young. This might be her own basket or a special birthing box. This must be ready at least a week before the birth to give the mother time to get used to it. The basket or box should preferably be in a quiet place.

Birth

The average litter counts three to five puppies. Make sure that your vet knows when the birth is imminent, as Bulldogs quite often have problems giving birth. Not all litters are born via a caesarean. There are, however, still vets who don't know that Bulldogs can give birth normally quite often. The bitch will be very emotional after giving birth. Never leave her alone with her puppies during the first few weeks. In an attempt to protect her puppies, she might gather them together and smother them.

Suckling and weaning

After giving birth, the mother starts to produce milk. The suckling period is very demanding. During the first three

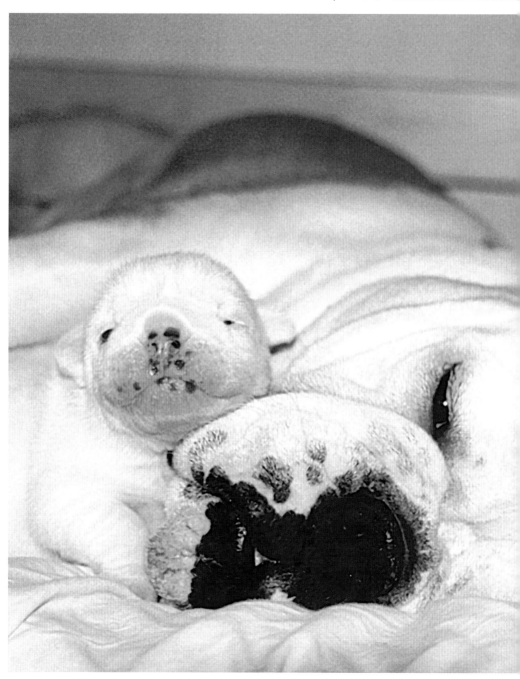

to four weeks the pups rely entirely on their mother's milk. During this time she needs extra food and fluids. This can be up to three or four times the normal amount. If she's producing too little milk, you can give both the mother and her young special puppy milk. Here too, divide the higher quantity of food the mother needs into several smaller portions. Again, choose a concentrated high-energy food and give her plenty of fresh drinking water. Do not give her cow's milk, as this can cause diarrhoea.

You can give the puppies some supplemental solid food when they are three to four weeks old. There are special puppy foods available that follow on well from the mother's milk, and that the puppies can easily eat with their milk teeth.

Ideally, the puppies are fully weaned at an age of six or seven weeks, i.e. they no longer drink their mother's milk. The mother's milk production gradually stops and her food needs also drop. Within a few weeks after weaning, the mother

should be back to getting the same amount of food as before the pregnancy.

Castration and sterilisation

As soon as you are sure that your bitch should never bear a (new) litter, a vasectomy or sterilisation is the best solution. During sterilisation (in fact this is normal castration) the uterus and the ovaries are removed in an operation. The bitch no longer goes into season and can never become pregnant. The best age for a sterilisation is about eighteen months, when she is more or less fully-grown.

A male dog is usually only castrated for medical reasons or to correct undesirable sexual behaviour. During a castration the testicles are removed, which is a simple procedure and usually without complications. There is no special age for castration but, where possible, wait until the dog is fully-grown. Vasectomy is sufficient where it's only a case of making the dog infertile. In this case the dog keeps its sexual drive but can no longer reproduce.

Shows

Bulldogs will not be happy with just going round the block once in a while, especially when they are young. They will get bored and will start to behave badly at home.

If you want to keep your young Bulldog happy, you will have to do something with it!

Dog shows

Visiting a dog show is a pleasant experience for both dog and master, and for some dog-lovers it has become a hobby. They visit countless shows every year. Others find it nice to visit an exemption show with their dog just once. It's worth making the effort to visit an exemption show where a judge's experienced eyes will inspect your Bulldog and assess it for form, condition and behaviour. The judge's report will teach you your dog's weak and strong points, which may help you when choosing a mate for breeding. You can also exchange experiences with other Bulldog owners. Official shows are only open to dogs with pedigrees.

Ring training

If you've never been to an exemption show, you're probably tapping in the dark in terms of what will be expected of you and your dog. Many kennel clubs organise so-called ring training courses for dogs going to an exemption show for the first time. This training teaches you exactly what the judge will be looking for, and you can practise the correct techniques together with your dog.

Club matches

Almost all kennel clubs organise club matches. You have to enter your dog in a certain class before the big day. These meetings are usually small and friendly and are often the first acquaintance dog and master make with a judge. This is an overwhelming experience for your dog - a lot of its contemporaries and a strange man or woman who fiddles around with it and peers into its mouth. After a few times, your dog will know exactly what's expected of it and will happily go to the next club match.

Championship shows

Various championship shows take place during the course of the year, offering different prizes. These shows are much more strictly organised than club matches. Here too, your dog must be registered in a certain class in advance and it will then be listed in a catalogue. On the day itself, the dog is kept in a cage (indoor kennel) until its turn comes up. During the judging in the ring, it's important that you show your dog at its best. The judge will give an official verdict and write a report. When all the dogs from that class have been judged, the winner is selected. You can pick up your report, and possibly your prize, after the class has finished.

The winners of the various classes will then compete for the title of Best of Breed. A winner will be chosen from the dogs belonging to the same breed group. The various winners of the different breed groups will then compete for Best in Show.

Your dog must be in top condition for a show. This means that you must have paid attention to your dog's appearance well in advance. Get information from more experienced exhibitors or the breed association. The judge will not be pleased if your dog's coat is dirty and its paws covered in mud. Its nails must be clipped and the teeth free of tartar. The dog must also not have any parasites or illnesses.

A bitch must not be in season, and a dog should have both its testicles. Judges also don't like badly raised, frightened or nervous dogs. If you want to know more about shows, contact your kennel club or the breed association.

Don't forget!

If you plan to visit a show with your Bulldog, you need to be well prepared. You must certainly not forget the following:

For yourself:
- Registration card
- Food and drink
- Safety pin for the catalogue number
- Chair(s)

For your dog:
- Food and drink bowls and food
- Dog blanket and perhaps a cushion
- Show lead
- A brush
- Some chalk to clean its coat

Parasites

All dogs are vulnerable to various sorts of parasite. Parasites are tiny creatures that live at the expense of another animal. They feed on blood, skin and other body substances.

There are two main types. Internal parasites live within their host animal's body (tapeworm and roundworm); external parasites live on the animal's exterior, usually in its coat (fleas and ticks), but also in its ears (ear mite).

Fleas

Fleas feed on a dog's blood. They cause not only itching and skin problems, but can also carry infections such as tapeworm. In large numbers they can cause anaemia and dogs can also become allergic to a flea's saliva, which can cause serious skin conditions.

So it's important that you treat your dog for fleas as effectively as possible. Do not just treat the animal itself, but also its surroundings. To treat your dog, there are various medicines: drops for the neck and to put in its food, flea collars, long-life sprays and flea powders. There are various sprays on sale in pet shops, which can be used to eradicate fleas in the dog's immediate surroundings. Choose a spray that kills both adult fleas and their larvae. If your dog goes in your car, you should spray that too.

Fleas can also affect other pets, so you should treat those too. When spraying a room, cover any aquarium or fishbowl. If the spray reaches the water, it can be fatal for your fish!

Your vet and pet shop have a wide range of flea treatments and can advise you on the subject.

Ticks

Ticks are small, spider-like parasites. They feed on the blood of the animal or person they've attached to. A tick looks like a tiny, grey leather bag with eight feet. When it has sucked itself full, it is darker in colour and can easily be five to ten times its own size.

Dogs usually fall victim to ticks in bushes, woods or long grass. Ticks cause not only irritation by their blood-sucking, but can also carry a number of serious diseases. This applies especially to the Mediterranean countries, which can be infested with blood parasites. In our country these diseases are fortunately less common, but Lyme disease, which can also affect humans, has reached our shores. Your vet can prescribe a special treatment if you're planning to take your dog to southern Europe.

It is important to fight ticks as effectively as possible. Check your dog regularly, especially if it's been running free in woods and bushes. It can also wear an anti-tick collar. Removing a tick is simple using tick tweezers. Grip the tick with the tweezers as close to the dog's skin as possible, and carefully pull it out. You can also grip the tick between your fingers and, using a turning movement, pull it carefully out. You must disinfect the spot where the tick had been, using iodine to prevent infection. Never soak the tick in alcohol, ether or oil. In a shock reaction, it may discharge the infected contents of its stomach into the dog's skin.

Worms

Dogs can suffer from various types of worm. The most common are tapeworm and roundworm. Tapeworm causes diarrhoea and poor condition. With a tapeworm infection you can sometimes find small pieces of the worm around the dog's anus or on its bed. In this case, your dog must be wormed. You should also check your dog for fleas, as these can carry the tapeworm infection.

Roundworm is a condition that reoccurs regularly. Puppies are often infected by their mother's milk. Roundworm causes problems (particularly in younger dogs), such as diarrhoea, loss of weight and stagnated growth. In serious cases the pup becomes thin, but with a swollen belly. It may vomit and you can then see the worms in its vomit. They are spaghetti-like tendrils. In its first year, a puppy needs to be treated every three months with a worm treatment. Adult dogs should be treated every six months.

Tick

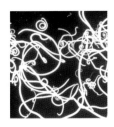

Roundworms

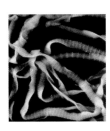

Tapeworms

Your Bulldog's health

It is important to know a little bit more about the possible heath problems of your dog.

There is not enough room in this book to deal with all the medical ups and downs of the Bulldog. We will limit ourselves to dealing with some illnesses and abnormalities, which are more common with the Bulldog than with any other breed.

Breed-specific ailments

The Bulldog was famous in the past for its bad health and its strained, often snoring, breathing. This had two causes: Firstly, the Bulldog had too much skin at its throat. The folds caused snoring sounds to develop in the dog's throat. Secondly, its windpipe was often too narrow, which meant that the dog was breathing as if through a straw, and easily became short of breath. The first condition could be operated on, whereas the second was often fatal.

The breed association noticed the need to solve this problem by excluding affected dogs from breeding. Over the last decade, breeders who followed the rules of the breed association have created a healthy population. There are still some Bulldogs that discharge froth from their mouths, especially when they feel under pressure. The problem has, however, almost disappeared thanks to the above breeding programme.

Nodules between the toes

Another typical Bulldog problem, which is very difficult to treat, is the development of nodules between the toes. This condition is particularly common with Bulldogs with fleshy feet, which might sag slightly. The skin between the toes reaches the ground, which causes abrasions and bruising. This can be the stimulus for an inflammation process. The skin between the toes swells, and the dog's licking can cause the nodules to burst open. This relieves the tension, and the Bulldog is no longer bothered by it.

Cherry eye

The third eyelid is a nictitating membrane under the eyelids. Beginning from the inside corner of the eye, it closes over the whole eye as a protective layer. A gland is located on the third eyelid. If it does not function or becomes irritated, the third eyelid and the gland can become inflamed and are then visible as a nodule in the inside corner of the eye. This is called a 'Cherry Eye' due to its red colour and the shape. Some bloodlines are more susceptible to this condition than others, so a genetic factor probably contributes to it.

Entropion

Entropion occurs regularly with the Bulldog. Entropion is a condition where the eyelid curls to the inside, so that the hairs from the coat irritate the eyeball. The dog blinks a lot and the eyes water constantly. Surgical correction is necessary with this condition.

Tips for the Bulldog

- Buy your Bulldog from a reputable breeder via the breed association.
- Visit several breeders before selecting a puppy.
- Always ask for the parent animals' health certificates. The parents must not have any hereditary abnormalities. The eyes must have been examined for entropion and ectropion.
- Make a purchase contract with the breeder when buying your puppy.
- Join a puppy training course with your puppy. It teaches both dog and owner a lot.
- Do not let your Bulldog climb up stairs for the first six months.
- Its first journey is quite an adventure for a puppy. Make sure it's a nice one!

- Never buy a puppy whose mother you weren't able to see.
- Hard, dry food and chewing material will keep your dog's teeth healthy.
- Never give your Bulldog cowhide or buffalo hide chews, as they can cause suffocation.
- Make sure that your dog doesn't become overweight. Not too much food and plenty of exercise are the golden rules.
- Never leave a dog alone with small children.
- Do not let your puppy run endlessly after a ball or stick.
- Do not only treat fleas, but also their larvae.
- Organise a holiday home or a dog-sitter for your Bulldog well in advance.

Breed clubs

Join a breed club. It will help you with tips and advice, and also organises lots of fun activities.

Bath & Western Counties Bulldog Club
Sec. Mrs A Godwin
Tel No: 0117 9374033

Birmingham & Midland Counties Bulldog Club
Sec. Mr A M Darmanin
Tel No: 01630 638856

Blackpool & Fylde Bulldog Club
Sec. Mr P Reynolds
Tel No: 01782 510774

British Bulldog Club
Sec. Ms Aldridge
www.britishbulldogclub.co.uk

Bulldog Club (Incorporated)
Mr. C. Carberry
Tel/Fax: 01327 855835
Email: bulldogclubinc.
secretaryeditor@virgin.net
www.bulldog-inc.com

Bulldog Club Of Scotland
Sec. Mrs S Rowe
Tel No: 01228 576424

Bulldog Club Of Wales
Sec. Mr J Lane
Tel No: 01222 734631

Caledonian Bulldog Club
Sec. Mrs M Wyse
Tel No: 01592 261017
http://members.lycos.co.uk/
dennypops/indexc.htm

East Midland Bulldog Club
Sec. Mrs Y A Franklin
Tel No: Not available
for more information contact the
Kennel Club

Junior Bulldog Club
Sec. Mr Presland
Tel No: 01684 273017
Leodensian Bulldog Club
Sec. Mrs V Williams
Tel No: 01302 845670

London Bulldog Society
Sec. Miss S A Jay
Tel No: 020 8777 0198

**Manchester & Counties Bulldog
Club**
Sec. Mrs M Williams
Tel No: 01244 547226

Northern Bulldog Club
Sec. Mr D Rodgers
Tel No: 01942 707170

**Northumberland & Durham
Bulldog Club**
Sec. Mrs Grieves
Tel No: 01670 774418

**Plymouth, Devon & Cornwall
Bulldog Club**
Sec. Mr J Smith
Tel No: 01452 721389

**Rochdale & District Bulldog
Club**
Sec. Mrs A Prescott
Tel No: 0151 531 8850

**Sheffield & District Bulldog
Club**
Sec. Mrs Evison
Tel No: 01283 762220

**South Of England Bulldog
Society**
Sec. Mrs L Manns
Tel No: 01329 847005

Yorkshire Bulldog Club
Sec. Mrs Revis
Tel No: 01302 846958

The Bulldog

Origin:	Great Britain
FCI-classification:	Group 2: Pinchers and Schnauzers, Molossers and Swiss mountain dogs
Breed association established:	1985
Original task:	Bull baiting
Present task:	Companion dog
Character:	Friendly
Weight:	Bitch: 22.7 kg (50 lbs) Dog: 25 kg (55 lbs)
Life expectancy:	9 to 11 years